Improving
ENDURANCE

Paul Mason

WAYLAND

First published in 2010 by Wayland

Copyright © Wayland 2010

Wayland
Hachette Children's Books
338 Euston Road
London NW1 3BH

Wayland Australia
Level 17/207 Kent Street
Sydney, NSW 2000

Editor: Julia Adams
Designer: Tim Mayer, Mayer Media
Picture Researcher: Kathy Lockley
Proofreader and indexer: Claire Shanahan
Consultant: Professor John Brewer

British Library Cataloguing in Publication Data
Mason, Paul, 1967-
   Training for sport.
   Endurance.
   1. Physical fitness--Juvenile literature. 2. Physical
   fitness--Nutritional aspects--Juvenile literature.
   I. Title
   613.7'1-dc22

ISBN 9780750261418

Printed in China

Wayland is a division of Hachette Children's Books,
an Hachette UK company.
www.hachette.co.uk

Websites

The website addresses (URLs) included in this book were
valid at the time of going to press. However, because of the
nature of the Internet, it is possible that some addresses may
have changed, or sites may have changed or closed down
since publication. While the author and publisher regret any
inconvenience this may cause the readers, no responsibility
for any such changes can be accepted by either the author
or the publisher.

Disclaimer
During the preparation of this book, all due care has been
taken with regard to the advice, activities and techniques
described and depicted. The publishers regret that they can
accept no liability for any loss or injury sustained.

Picture acknowledgements:
AdrianHillman/iStock images: folios throughout
AP/AP/Press Association Images: 27
Chris Cheadle/All Canada Photos/Getty Images: 4
Loetscher Chlaus/Alamy: 20
Thomas Coex/AFP/Getty Images:21
Rob Crandall/Alamy: 8CL
Luis Davilla/Cover/Getty Images: 14
Aaron Francis/Getty Images: 10
Global Warming Images/Alamy: title page, 23
Anton Hlushchenko/Shutterstock: COVER (small, middle)
Image Source/Getty Images: 18
Jed Jacobsohn/Getty Images: 17TR
John Kelly/The Image Bank/Getty Images: COVER (main)
Bryn Lennon/Getty Images: 7
Victor Lerena/epa/Corbis: 8-9B
Indranil Mukherjee/AFP/Getty Images: 22
Vitalii Nesterchuk/Shutterstock: COVER (small, top)
PhotoSky 4t com/Shutterstock: background throughout
Mike Powell/ALLSPORT/Getty Images: 13, 19
Adam Pretty/Getty Images: 6
Frances M. Roberts/Alamy: 25TR
StockShot/Alamy: 28
T-Design/Shutterstock: background throughout
Stanislaw Tokarski/Shutterstock: COVER (small, bottom)
© 2004 TopFoto, TopFoto.co.uk: 15
Tim de Waele/Corbis: 5, 16-17B, 26
Gordon Wiltsie/National Geographic/Getty Images: 24-25B
Dmitry Yashkin/Shutterstock: background throughout

Contents

What is endurance?

Imagine you're on your bike, at the bottom of a hill. It's a steep hill, but you just shift to an easier gear, and keep pedalling. At the top, you shift back and carry on at the same speed. You're not even out of breath. Being able to keep going like that, hill after hill, is called endurance.

The human machine

Think of your body as a machine. Like all machines, it needs fuel to make it go. In the human machine, this fuel comes from food. In endurance sports, the fuel combines with oxygen, which is breathed in via your lungs. This combination of fuel and oxygen provides your muscles with energy.

Long-distance machine

For your body to have good endurance, it needs to keep providing your muscles with the energy to carry on working. The energy your body uses has to be replaced. Otherwise, your ability to keep going drops. You'll be like a toy car whose batteries are running flat.

These triathletes are about to swim 1500 metres, cycle 40 kilometres and run 10 kilometres.

4

Limerick
County Library

Energy-efficient technique

Top endurance athletes aim to use the minimum amount of energy possible. They do this by making their technique efficient. Imagine an old-fashioned steam train, huffing and puffing, and losing energy all the time. That's no good! You need to be like a modern electric train, gliding along without obvious effort, wasting as little energy as possible.

The good news is that everyone can train to improve their endurance, and this book will help you find out how that happens.

Lance Armstrong races uphill on a mountainous stage of the Tour de France.

Endurance sports

Endurance sports are ones where the athlete performs at less than maximum speed, but for a long time. For any race that lasts longer than a minute, athletes need to train for endurance. As the race time and distance get greater, the need for endurance, rather than outright speed, also becomes more important.

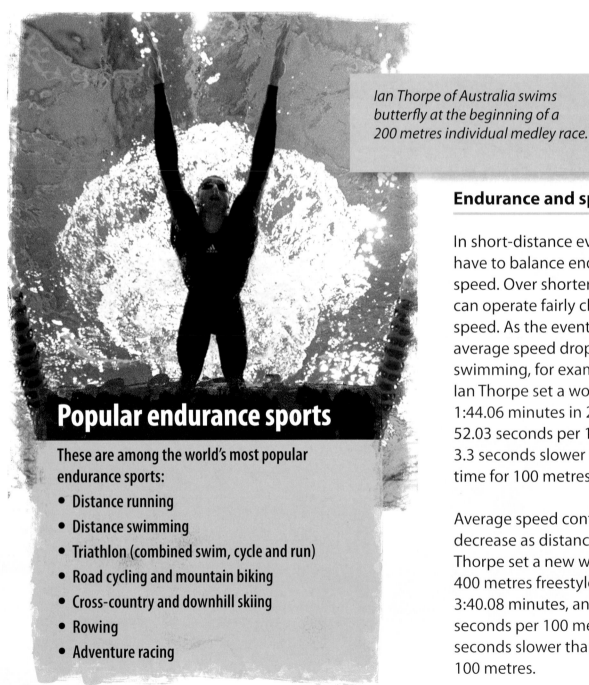

Ian Thorpe of Australia swims butterfly at the beginning of a 200 metres individual medley race.

Popular endurance sports

These are among the world's most popular endurance sports:

- Distance running
- Distance swimming
- Triathlon (combined swim, cycle and run)
- Road cycling and mountain biking
- Cross-country and downhill skiing
- Rowing
- Adventure racing

Endurance and speed

In short-distance events, athletes have to balance endurance against speed. Over shorter distances, they can operate fairly close to their top speed. As the events get longer, their average speed drops. In 200 metres swimming, for example, Australia's Ian Thorpe set a world record of 1:44.06 minutes in 2001. That's 52.03 seconds per 100 metres – 3.3 seconds slower than his best time for 100 metres.

Average speed continues to decrease as distances grow. In 2002 Thorpe set a new world record for 400 metres freestyle. His time was 3:40.08 minutes, an average of 55.02 seconds per 100 metres. This was 6.3 seconds slower than his best time for 100 metres.

Pure endurance

In endurance races, athletes may be competing for hours, days, or even weeks. The need for top speed is outweighed by the need for excellent endurance. Their average times are some way off their best times over shorter distances, but they are able to keep up a high average speed for extremely long periods. In the 2005 *Tour de France*, for example, winner Lance Armstrong averaged 41.65 kilometres per hour over three weeks' racing!

Paula Radcliffe winning the world half-marathon championship in 2003.

Paula Radcliffe

Sport: Distance running

Country: UK

Born: 17 December 1973

Paula Radcliffe is one of the most successful female distance runners ever seen. In the early days of her career, though, she had a long, painful history of missing out on medals in major races. Athletes with a faster finish kept zooming past her at the end of the race.

Then, in 2001, Radcliff made a breakthrough. At the world cross-country championships, she outsprinted her rival Gete Wami in the last 50 metres. In 2002, she won the world cross-country championships, the London marathon, and the Chicago marathon.

Between February and September 2003, Radcliff set world record times for 10 km and 20 km road races, and the marathon. Her marathon world record of 2.15.25 hours was over 3 minutes faster than any other female runner. It remains one of the greatest endurance records ever set.

Endurance athletes

Everyone can train to improve their endurance. We don't all start from the same place, though. Some people are born with a body shape and muscles that are particularly good for taking part in endurance sports. If you look at a group of marathon runners, for example, you will see that most will have a very similar body shape: small and slim.

Body shape

We are all born with a basic body shape that we cannot change. There are three extremes of shape:
1) endomorphs – stocky people, who often have large, powerful muscles
2) ectomorphs – thinner people, who tend to have smaller, slimmer muscles
3) mesomorphs – wide-shouldered and slim-hipped people; they combine the characteristics of endomorphs and ectomorphs.

In general, endomorphs are best at strength-based sports. Mesomorphs are best able to combine speed and endurance. Endurance sportspeople are usually ectomorphs.

Muscle types

In humans, there are two main types of muscle fibre:
1) fast-twitch muscle fibres. These are able to quickly generate power, but they also quickly use up energy. This means they are good for short, fast events, but not for endurance.

2) slow-twitch muscle fibres. These generate power more slowly, but are good at using oxygen to provide energy. They are able to repeat movements again and again without becoming fatigued. Slow twitch muscles are ideal for endurance events.

Everyone is born with a different proportion of fast-twitch and slow-twitch muscle fibres. People with a higher number of slow-twitch muscle fibres are best suited to endurance events.

These bike riders are just starting a race that will last several hours. The winner will need excellent endurance.

Gunn-Rita Dahle-Flesjå

Sport: Cross-country mountain biking

Country: Norway

Born: 10 February 1973

Gunn-Rita Dahle-Flesjå is the most successful female cross-country mountain biker ever. Cross-country races are held on off-road trails that climb and dip through the countryside. The changes in terrain make it tricky for the riders: they are constantly slowing down, then racing to get back up to speed. Races are typically about 40 km long.

Unlike many top athletes, Dahle-Flesjå discovered her sport late: she was 22 when she first rode a mountain bike. Within two months she had won the Norwegian championships. Four months after that, she became a professional rider.

Between 2002 and 2006, Dahle-Flesjå won six world championships and six European championships. She also won the mountain-bike gold medal at the 2004 Olympic Games. In 2003, 2004, 2005 and 2006, she won the UCI World Cup, a competition based on points earned in top-level races through the whole racing season.

Gunn-Rita Dahle-Flesjå (on the far right) at the start of a World Cup race in Spain. As so often, she went on to win.

9

Training the heart

Whenever you do hard exercise, your heart starts beating more quickly. It's rushing to pump oxygen from your lungs to your muscles, which are suddenly demanding a lot more energy! Once oxygen reaches the muscles, it reacts with a substance called ATP. ATP is sometimes called the body's 'energy currency'. Oxygen allows ATP to release energy, helping the muscles to do their work.

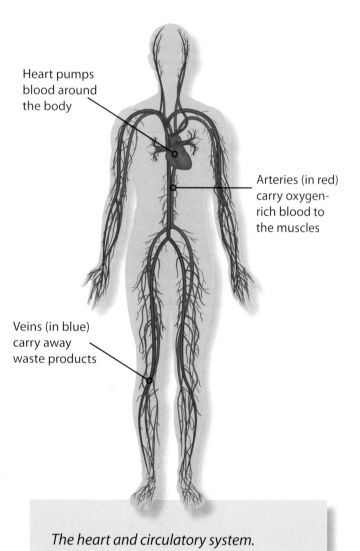

Heart pumps blood around the body

Arteries (in red) carry oxygen-rich blood to the muscles

Veins (in blue) carry away waste products

The heart and circulatory system.

Training for a healthy heart

A strong, efficient heart is crucial for endurance athletes. They need their heart in good shape so that it can keep pumping plenty of oxygen-rich blood around the body for long periods. Unless it can do this, ATP does not keep releasing energy, and the muscles are not able to do their work.

Heart rate

The number of times your heart beats each minute is called your heart rate. Measuring how quickly heart rate returns to normal after exercise is a good measure of how fit people are. This is called their recovery rate. To test this:

- measure resting heart rate (heart rate before exercise)

- take your heart rate as soon as exercise is finished

- take your heart rate one minute after finishing.

Very fit athletes' hearts will slow by 50–60 beats in the minute. The average person would slow by about 30 beats in the minute. Less than that and you are really not very fit!

Heart-rate monitors

Many sportspeople now use heart-rate monitors (HRMs) in training. These little computers can be carried while training, and measure the heart rate exactly. Athletes train at different percentages of their maximum heart rate (MHR), depending on what they want to achieve:

- 60–70 per cent of MHR
  Improves endurance and recovery: body becomes more efficient at feeding working muscles, and better learns to use fat as a fuel source.

- 70–80 per cent of MHR
  Increases fitness of heart and lungs; improves transport of oxygen to muscles and waste products away.

- 80–90 per cent of MHR
  Delays the point at which your body can no longer transport away waste products.

- 90 per cent plus
  Even expert athletes only train in this zone for short periods: develops strength and speed.

These runners are using heart-rate monitors (HRM) as part of their training. At home, they will be able to download the information into a training diary.

Calculating maximum heart rate

Top sportspeople have their MHR scientifically measured, but there are several ways to work out your estimated MHR. The simplest is to use this formula:

$$MHR = 220 - your\ age$$

So if you are 15, your maximum heart rate is $220 - 15 = 205$ heartbeats per minute.

Various alternative formulae to this have been suggested, including this one from Indiana University in 1993:

$$MHR = 217 - (0.85 \times your\ age)$$

So, a 15-year-old would have an MHR of $217 - (0.85 \times 15) = 204.25$ heartbeats per minute.

The Indiana formula produces bigger differences with older athletes. For example, it produces an MHR for a 40-year-old of 183, compared with 180 using the traditional method.

Training the lungs

Why do you start breathing harder if you run up a hill? It's because your muscles are asking for extra energy, and to get it they need oxygen. Oxygen is breathed in through the respiratory system. From the lungs it is absorbed into your blood. Then your heart pumps the oxygen-rich blood to the muscles. Without healthy lungs, this process does not work properly.

Healthy lungs

What makes someone's lungs healthy? They need to be able to:

- take in as much air as possible. The amount of air your lungs can take in is known as your lung capacity.

- transmit oxygen from the air into the bloodstream as effectively as possible.

- breathe out waste gases, particularly carbon dioxide.

It is important that the lining of the lungs is as clean as possible, otherwise these processes become less effective. This is why smokers feel out of breath more quickly than non-smokers. Smoking coats the lung lining with tar. The tar forms a barrier to oxygen trying to enter the bloodstream.

Lungs for endurance

Lungs are a crucial part of the supply chain of energy for endurance athletes. A lot of endurance training is done at 70–80 per cent of maximum heart rate, because this is where the respiratory and cardiac systems get the most benefit:

- the ability of the lungs to extract oxygen from air (and to expel waste gas) improves

- the muscles that control breathing become stronger and more flexible: the lungs can breathe more rapidly, and they become more elastic

- the body is stimulated to build new blood vessels, which help transport oxygen-rich blood to the muscles and carry away waste products.

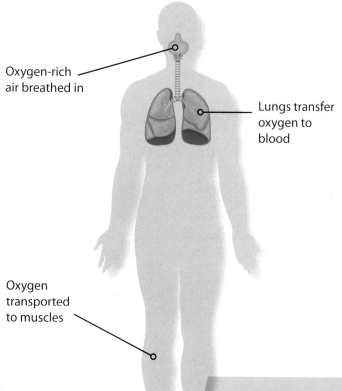

Oxygen-rich air breathed in

Lungs transfer oxygen to blood

Oxygen transported to muscles

The respiratory system.

Miguel Indurain heads uphill during the Tour de France. *His respiratory system was so efficient that he often rode with his mouth closed, breathing only through his nose.*

Miguel Indurain

Sport: Road cycling

Country: Spain

Born: 16 July 1964

Miguel Indurain was an outstanding road-racing cyclist. He was famous for his physical advantages over other riders, including lungs that were a third bigger than an ordinary person's!

Between 1991 and 1995, Indurain dominated the *Tour de France*, winning it every year. He was the first person to win the *Tour* five years in a row, a feat only matched (and then bettered) by Lance Armstrong. In 1992 and 1993, Indurain also won the Giro d'Italia, the Italian equivalent of the *Tour de France* – Armstrong never won any of the other major tours.

Like all road racers, Indurain trained hard and was extremely fit. He also had unusual physical gifts:
- lungs with a capacity of 8 litres (compared to the usual 6 litres)
- the ability to pump 7 litres of oxygen around his body (compared to 3–4 for an ordinary person, or 6 for other professional cyclists)
- a heart that could pump 50 litres of blood per minute (double the amount of a fit amateur cyclist)
- a resting heart rate of 29 beats per minute.

Aerobic exercise

Aerobic means 'with oxygen'. During aerobic exercise, the body is able to take in enough oxygen to keep producing energy for the muscles. The human body stores energy that it gets from food in the form of carbohydrate and fat. But without enough oxygen, the body cannot use these energy stores for long periods of time.

Energy sources

In aerobic exercise, the body starts by using carbohydrate, which is stored in the muscles and liver as a substance called glycogen. The glycogen provides the body with ATP, its 'energy currency'.

After roughly 1–2 hours, the body's glycogen stores are mostly used up, unless they have been topped up by eating and drinking.

Then the body starts to use glucose (another carbohydrate) from the bloodstream, plus increasing amounts of fat, as sources of energy.

VO2 and VO2 max

VO2 is a measure of the amount of oxygen the body uses. VO2 is expressed as the number of millilitres of oxygen used per kilogramme of body mass each minute. This is usually written as ml/kg. Just staying alive, sitting still, requires a VO2 of 3.5 ml/kg. Movement requires more oxygen, and therefore a higher VO2.

This athlete is connected to a machine that will accurately measure the maximum amount of oxygen his body can provide per hour (VO2 max).

VO2 max is the maximum amount of oxygen a person's body can provide per hour. Most people have a VO2 max of about 20 ml/kg. Top endurance athletes tend to have a VO2 max three to four times this, of 60–80 ml/kg.

Relative intensity

Relative intensity is a way of describing how close to their VO2 max sportspeople are able to stay for long periods. Someone who runs seriously, but mainly for enjoyment, would normally be able to run a marathon at about 65per cent of their VO2 max. Top marathon runners, who train to improve the intensity at which they can operate, race at roughly 80 per cent of VO2 max.

Alison Streeter set the world record in 1992 by swimming the channel seven times in one season. She completed one crossing every 10 days.

PROFESSIONAL PROFILE

Alison Streeter

Sport: Long-distance sea swimming

Country: UK

Born: 1964

Alison Streeter MBE is known as 'Queen of the English Channel'. She has swum the Channel, the stretch of water between England and France, more times than anyone else. By 2009, Streeter had made the crossing an amazing 43 times.

At its shortest, the Channel is just over 30 km across. But swimmers cannot swim in a dead-straight line, because they are pushed to and fro by waves, tides and currents. Most people end up swimming a lot further, and are usually in the cold water for between 10 and 16 hours. Cold water poses a big challenge for the swimmers. Body fat helps keep them warm, so they rarely have the same slim shape as other endurance athletes.

As well as breaking Channel swimming records, Streeter has made many other amazing long-distance swims:

- 100 km around the Isle of Wight in 21 hours 2 minutes
- first person to swim from Scotland to Ireland
- round Manhattan in 6 hours 47 minutes.

Anaerobic exercise

Anaerobic means 'without oxygen'. During anaerobic exercise, the body is not able to provide enough oxygen for the muscles to work. The muscles have to get their energy in way that does not require oxygen to be present. Anaerobic energy production is very quick, and is ideal for events lasting up to 90 seconds.

Emptying the tank

Anaerobic exercise uses the body's glycogen, which is stored in the muscles. It uses glycogen in a very inefficient way. In anaerobic exercise, glycogen is broken down into glucose, which then produces ATP. Each glucose molecule produces two molecules of ATP. In comparison, in aerobic exercise the presence of oxygen means each glucose molecule produces 38 molecules of ATP. Anaerobic exercise empties the body's stores of glycogen very quickly, and cannot be kept going for long.

Lactic acid

Anaerobic energy production causes a build-up of lactic acid in the muscles. The increasing acidity makes it more and more difficult for the muscles to carry on working, and produces a feeling of soreness and fatigue.

Small amounts of lactic acid can be removed from the muscles during aerobic exercise. This is why it is possible to add a short burst of speed in the middle of an endurance race.

If the body is unable to switch back to aerobic energy production, the levels of lactic acid in the muscles continue to increase. High-level performance cannot then continue: the muscles cannot work properly and quickly feel fatigued.

In endurance races, starting too fast is a bad idea. It could cause a build-up of lactic acid in the muscles.

Lance attacks! Throughout his career, Lance Armstrong has been able to lose other riders by putting in a burst of speed on steep climbs, as he has a high lactic acid threshold.

Lactic threshold

The lactic threshold is the point at which lactic acid starts to build up in your muscles. (It is also called the anaerobic threshold.) For most people, the lactic threshold lies somewhere between 85–90 per cent of their maximum heart rate. This is why a healthy heart, able to pump at high speed, is important for endurance athletes.

- Someone whose heart can pump at 200 beats per minute would have a lactic threshold of roughly 170.

- Someone whose heart can pump at a maximum of 170 beats per minute has a lactic threshold of roughly 145.

With all other things equal, it is likely that the athlete with the higher lactic threshold will be able to keep exercising at a higher intensity without feeling as tired.

Warming up and cooling down

Warming up and cooling down are crucial parts of any athlete's training programme. It can be tempting to go straight into hard training, but 15–30 minutes of warm-up activity at the start is extremely important.

Benefits of warming up

The increased blood flow and raised muscle temperatures caused by warming up have several benefits:

- **More efficient oxygen use**
  Blood releases oxygen more easily at higher temperatures, so energy release to warmed-up muscles is more efficient.

- **Increased speed of movement**
  Warmed-up muscles are able to contract and relax more quickly. They have less resistance to movement. Signals to the muscle from the nervous system are faster at higher temperatures.

- **Preventing injury**
  Muscles that have not been stretched before being asked to do hard work are more likely to be damaged.

Warming Up

This is a typical general warm-up for a sportsperson. The details will depend on what sport people take part in.

- **Phase 1**
  Most athletes start their warm-up with some gentle activity. Five to 10 minutes of gentle exercise, at an easy pace, increases their heart rate and gets blood flowing more rapidly around the body.

- **Phase 2**
  The middle part of the warm-up is 5–10 minutes spent stretching key muscle groups. This helps reduce muscle stiffness.

- **Phase 3**
  Finally, athletes spend 5–10 minutes working on their technique, perhaps using drills. The pace of this phase of the warm-up is still gentle, but can be harder than phase 1.

Stretching as part of a warm-up helps reduce the chances of getting injured.

Cooling down

Cooling down after hard training or racing helps your body to recover more quickly. It gives your body a chance to start getting rid of any lactic acid, reduces the chances of your muscles later becoming sore, and allows your heart to return gently to its resting rate. Most athletes cool down using 5–10 minutes of gentle exercise, then 5–10 minutes of stretching.

Mark Allen grits his teeth on the way to yet another victory in the Ironman World Championship in Hawaii, this one in 1992.

Mark Allen

Sport: Ironman triathlon

Country: USA

Born: 12 January 1958

How would you like to be described as The Fittest Athlete In The World? That's the title given to Mark Allen, one of the toughest competitors in one of the toughest sports in the world – Ironman racing.

The first Ironman contest grew out of an argument in Hawaii over which were fittest: swimmers, cyclists or runners. To settle the debate, athletes from each sport set out to:

- swim the 3.86 km course of the Waikiki Roughwater Swim
- cycle 180.2 km of the Round Oahu Bike Race
- run the 42.2 km of the Honolulu Marathon.

The difference to other triathlons was that they completed them one after the other, all on the same day!

This race, now held on Hawaii's Big Island, is today famous as the Ironman World Championships, and Allen has won it six times. Equally impressive, he has won the famous Nice International Triathlon ten times.

19

Training for endurance

The aim of all endurance athletes is to improve the length of time for which they can maintain a high speed. There are many different ways of training. The type you rely on most depends on the kind of event for which you are training. Most athletes use a combination of continuous and interval training.

Continuous training

Continuous training is exactly what it sounds like: training in which the sportsperson runs, swims, cycles, or rows non-stop for a set period of time. By varying the length of time and intensity at which they exercise, athletes can achieve different outcomes:

- exercising at 50–60 per cent of MHR for over 60 minutes builds basic aerobic endurance. This easy pace is good for training for extreme distances, and might be used by ultra runners, for example (see p. 27).

- 60–70 per cent of MHR for 45–90 minutes, or 70–80 per cent of MHR for 30–45 minutes, improves the cardiovascular system and aerobic endurance, and might be used by marathon runners or 1500-metre swimmers, for example. The higher pace is more suitable for shorter events.

- 80–90 per cent of MHR for 10–20 minutes improves the cardiovascular system, lactic acid tolerance and its removal. It also promotes efficient use of muscle glycogen.

Long distances at a steady pace are a good way to build up the body's endurance.

Interval training

In interval training, sportspeople mix together higher speeds with slower ones and/or rests. This combination helps develop the body's ability to recover from hard efforts by increasing the strength of the heart, increasing the muscles' resistance to lactic acid, stimulating the growth of new blood vessels, and improving the transmission of oxygen to where it is needed.

Runners, swimmers and cyclists all rely on interval training to build endurance. In the pool, for example, a swimmer might do five 100-metre swims, starting each one 1 minute 20 seconds after the last. Then they would rest for a few minutes, before repeating the five 100 metres.

Steve Redgrave

Sport: Rowing

Country: UK

Born: 23 March 1962

Sir Steve Redgrave is the greatest competition rower of all time. He specialised in the coxless four and coxless pars races, which take place over 2000 metres.

The sport is almost unique in that, even though it takes six minutes to cover the course, the rowers must sprint at almost full speed for the first 500 metres. They ease off very slightly in the middle 1000 metres, before charging for the finish line again in the last 500. The demands on the body's aerobic and anaerobic energy systems, heart and lungs are extreme.

Redgrave's rowing achievements led many people to call him the athlete of the century. Nine times the world champion, he also won gold medals at every Olympic Games between 1984 and 2000. No other endurance athlete has dominated their sport for such a long period of time.

Steve Redgrave wins his fifth Olympic gold medal, at the 2000 Sydney Olympics.

Recovery

For all sportspeople, recovery from the efforts of training and racing is crucial. This is especially so in multi-day events, such as bicycle stage races and adventure races. Proper, planned recovery gives your body a chance to repair minor injuries and damage to muscle fibres, and to restock its energy supplies.

English cricketer Andrew Flintoff gets a massage. Massage increases blood flow and helps the muscles to recover from effort.

Light exercise to recover

Doing some light exercise, rather than resting completely, helps your body to recover more quickly. Working at an easy aerobic level (60–65 per cent of MHR) increases the flow of blood. This means nutrients reach the muscles faster, renewing their energy stores and helping to repair any damage. Faster blood flow also decreases muscle acidity more quickly.

Food, drink and recovery

One of the main priorities in recovering from endurance events is to replace the muscle glycogen that has been used up during exercise. This process can take up to 20 hours, but it is possible to get a head start in the 15–30 minutes after you finish exercising. By taking carbohydrate-rich food and drink during this time, you start topping up your muscles' energy stores in the most efficient way.

If the food or drink also has protein in it, this helps recovery in two ways. First, the protein stimulates even more effective glycogen replacement. Second, the protein helps repair broken-down muscle tissue.

This all sounds complicated, but it isn't: for an athlete weighing about 70 kg, a whole wheat bagel with chicken or beef in it will do the job.

Recovery drinks

Everyone sweats during hard exercise, and they don't only lose water. Their bodies also lose minerals called electrolytes, which are crucial in the process of contracting and relaxing muscles. Replacing these electrolytes after hard exercise is important. Fruit juices and specialist sports drinks help your body to do this more effectively than plain water.

The top of a climb is only halfway – this mountaineer still has to get home safely before he can start to rest and recover.

Sleep

An irreplaceable part of the recovery process, sleeping allows your body to concentrate on restoring itself. Endurance athletes need at least eight hours sleep each 24 hours. Younger athletes, who are still growing, as well as trying to recover from exercise, need about 10 hours sleep in 24 hours (afternoon naps count as part of the total).

Nutrition for endurance training

An endurance athlete's body needs fuel to keep it going – and not just any fuel. You wouldn't try to run a MotoGP bike on lawn mower fuel. In the same way, you can't be a top-level endurance athlete and run on burgers and chips. Getting the right food and drink, at the right time, helps make sure that sportspeople get the maximum possible benefit from their training.

Nutrients

For the body to work, it needs nutrients, which it gets from food and drink. There are three main types of nutrient: carbohydrates (the main source of energy), fats (a second source of energy), and proteins (which help the body grow and repair itself). Other nutrients include minerals and vitamins, which are crucial to many of the body's functions.

Balancing these elements in an athlete's diet is important: they need to get enough of each nutrient for their body to function as well as possible.

The evening before a big race, runners eat huge bowls of pasta. They call this 'carb loading' – storing up easily accessible energy from carbohydrates, which can be burned off the next day (see p. 26).

Carbohydrate – a key energy source

Carbohydrates provide the body with glycogen, the energy store that is held in muscles and the liver. Glycogen is the body's key energy source during exercise, so endurance athletes must make sure they consume enough carbohydrate. Most aim for carbohydrate to make up 60–65 per cent of their calorie intake, a slightly higher proportion than other people. The rest of their intake is made up of roughly twice as much fat as protein.

Simple vs. complex carbohydrates

There are two types of carbohydrate: simple and complex. Simple carbohydrates are found in sweets, cakes, biscuits, puddings, soft drinks, jam and honey. Complex carbohydrates are found in potatoes, rice, bread, yoghurt, semi-skimmed milk, vegetables, beans and pulses. Both types can be used to replace glycogen. Complex carbohydrates are much lower in fat, and contain vitamins and minerals; they also release energy more steadily. Complex carbohydrates are the best type for endurance events.

How much food is enough?

Endurance athletes must get enough food for their body to function properly, and to provide energy for training and recovery. But most want to keep their weight as low as possible. How do they work out how many calories of food energy they need? This information can be used to find an answer:

- Basic energy requirement for the body to function = 1.3 calories per kg weight per hour
- Extra energy requirement for an hour's training = 8.5 calories per kg weight per hour.

So, a 70 kg athlete who trains for 3 hours a day has a basic energy requirement of 2184 calories every 24 hours (1.3 x 70 x 24), and an extra energy requirement of 1785 calories (8.5 x 70 x 3). They need to consume a total of 3969 calories a day. These basic figures make it possible to work out roughly how many calories food contains:

- 1 gram of carbohydrate = 4 calories
- 1 gram of fat = 9 calories
- 1 gram of protein = 4 calories.

Endurance athletes training together. If they are out for a long run, their backpacks will contain food and drink.

Nutrition for endurance competitions

How and what you eat in the days and hours leading up to an endurance race, and during it, will decide how well you do. Even the best-trained athletes cannot perform as well as possible unless they eat and drink properly at competition time.

Carb loading

During an endurance race, sportspeople make big demands on their body's stores of glycogen. The body gets glycogen from carbohydrates, so two or three days ahead of the event, the athletes start 'carb loading', eating large amounts of carbohydrates. Cereals, pasta, potatoes, lentils and rice are all popular, mixed with lean meat, chicken or fish to provide protein. This allows their body to store extra glycogen.

Pre-race food

On the day of the race, athletes eat a big meal about 3 hours ahead of the start time. This is their final chance to back up their glycogen stores, so they eat complex carbohydrates such as pasta or rice, perhaps with an egg or some cheese on top. If your start time is 11.00 am, this can make for a strange breakfast – but without it, you won't perform as well!

Forty minutes ahead of the start, experienced racers eat a banana, some dried fruit or a specially made energy bar, and drink about a third of a litre of sports drink. This ensures that when the race starts they will have some fuel in their stomach.

Eating while racing

In races lasting more than an hour or two, athletes need to eat regularly to top up their glycogen stores, which will be getting steadily lower. Eating something every hour or so is best: energy bars, fruit, flapjack and cookies are all popular snacks. For longer events, some athletes even make a sandwich and cut it into small triangles, then wrap them individually to take along. In top-level races there are usually 'feeding stations' where the racers can stock up on food.

German cyclist Jan Ullrich collects a musette – a food bag – from a feeding station during the Tour de France.

'Hitting the wall'

If athletes get their race food wrong, they end up 'hitting the wall' – running out of energy. The symptoms are:

- dizziness, heavy legs and lack of power, then;
- headache and nausea, then;
- hallucinations.

If athletes feel these symptoms start to come on, they need to eat some simple carbohydrates: energy bars, bananas or biscuits. These release energy quickly, and get glycogen to the muscles. This is only a short-term solution, though.

32-year-old Greek runner, Yiannis Kouros, a native of Tripolis, is seen at the end of the Sri Chimoy 1000-mile race in Flushing Meadows-Corona Park, New York, USA.

PROFESSIONAL PROFILE

Yiannis Kouros

Sport: Ultra running

Country: Greece

Born: 13 February 1956

Yiannis Kouros is a legend in the endurance sport of ultra running. Ultra running events take place over extreme distances or times. Technically, any running event longer than a marathon is an ultra run, but races are regularly held over 24 hours, 100 km or more.

At various times, Kouros has held world records for the following events:

- distance: 100-mile road, 1000-km road and track, 1000-km road, and 1000-mile road (in ten days, 10 hours!).
- time: 12-hour road and track, 24-hour road and track, 48-hour track, and 6-day road.

Kouros also won the Spartathlon race, between Athens and Sparta in Greece, four times. The race covers 246 km, and Kouros holds the four fastest times ever run.

Hydration

Hydration – providing your body with enough fluids – is almost as important for endurance athletes as nutrition. Without enough water, our bodies do not work properly. Drinking little and often is crucial to replace the fluid the body uses during exercise.

Hydration packs, which let you carry drinks in a backpack and suck them through a tube, are popular with fell runners, mountain bikers, skiers and snowboarders.

Sweating

When our muscles use energy, they generate heat. Our bodies sweat as a way of getting rid of some of that heat, stopping the body from overheating. People normally lose almost 3 litres of water a day from their bodies. Training or racing can easily double or even treble this amount. All that fluid needs to be replaced, or the body becomes dehydrated.

Dehydration

Dehydration can have severe effects. These become increasingly damaging as a larger percentage of the sportsperson's weight is lost through sweating:

Percentage of body weight lost:	Effect:
1–2 per cent	VO2 max decreases; thirst.
3–4 per cent	Ability for muscular activity declines; increased effort required.
5–6 per cent	Raised heart rate and breathing; reduced concentration; headache.
7–9 per cent	Dizziness, stumbling, confusion.
10+ per cent	Hallucinations; difficulty swallowing; risk of stroke and/or death.

Compare the colour of your urine with the colours on the chart to see if you're dehydrated or not!

Hydrated

Dehydrated

Dangerously dehydrated

Sweat rates

The amount people sweat in a set period of time is called their sweat rate. Sweat rates are influenced by various factors:

- gender: men tend to sweat more than women

- clothing: clothes that trap heat increase sweat rates

- air temperature and weather conditions: hot, humid, still days lead to higher sweat rates than cool, breezy ones

- percentage of MHR: exercising at a higher heart rate will increase sweating.

For all athletes, it is important to make sure that the fluids in their body are replaced at the same rate as they are lost through sweating. Water is not ideal for this, as it causes bloating and suppresses thirst – exactly what you don't need. Specialist sports drinks do the job more effectively.

Sports drinks

Many athletes buy pre-mixed powder that can be made into special drinks for sportspeople. There are three main kinds, which can be used for different purposes:

- Isotonic: these contain fluid, electrolytes and 6–8 per cent of carbohydrate. They replace the fluids and electrolytes lost in sweat, and give a boost of carbohydrate energy.

- Hypotonic: these contain fluid, electrolytes and a small amount of carbohydrate. They replace fluids and electrolytes, but do not give an energy boost.

- Hypertonic: these contain high levels of carbohydrate, so offer good glycogen replacement. If used during exercise, they need to be taken alongside isotonic drinks.

Rather than buying specialist isotonic drinks, it is possible to make your own. A little salt added to a mix of one-third fruit juice and two-thirds water does a similar job.

Glossary

adenosine triphoshate (ATP)
a chemical that provides living things with energy.

bloating
swelling, particularly of the stomach.

calorie
measure of the amount of energy contained in food.

cardiac
to do with the heart.

dehydrated
lacking water. In humans, dehydration can lead to lessened physical skills, confusion, sickness and even death.

drills
repeated movement designed to improve technique at a sport or physical activity.

efficient
done without wasting any energy.

fatigued
tired or worn out.

heart rate
speed at which the heart beats, measured in the number of beats per minute.

humid
containing a high level of moisture. A steamy bathroom after a hot shower is humid, for example.

intensity
amount of energy used.

lactic threshold
point during exercise at which lactic acid starts to build up in muscles. Also called the anaerobic threshold.

lung capacity
amount of air the lungs can hold.

nutrients
parts of food that allow a human body to work, and help it to grow and repair itself.

professional
paid to take part.

resistance
force that slows down another. The fluid inside muscles causes higher resistance to movement until it is warmed up.

respiratory
to do with breathing.

stages
parts of a multi-day endurance event. The word comes from cycling, in which each day's racing is known as a stage.

stroke
damage to a blood vessel in the brain, which can lead to permanent or temporary loss of movement, or even death.

terrain
ground or landscape, particularly its physical features. The word is often used when describing how hard a piece of ground is to cross. For example, someone might say: 'That's very rocky ground, so it will be difficult terrain to cross.'

VO2 max
the maximum amount of oxygen a person's body can provide per hour. VO2 max is expressed as the number of ml of oxygen used per kg of body mass each minute (ml/kg).

Further information

BOOKS TO READ

The Complete Guide to Endurance Training by Jon Ackland (A&C Black, 2004) The science of training for endurance, plus practical suggestions for training programmes that can be tailored to your own needs.

The Complete Guide To Sports Nutrition by Anita Bean (A&C Black, 2009) Everything you could want to know about food and drink for sports, including some excellent suggestions for meals.

Extreme! Secrets of Sport: The Technology That Makes Champions by James De Winter (A&C Black, 2008)

Goal! Science Projects With Soccer; Wheels! Science Projects With Bicycles, Skateboards and Skates by Madeline Goodstein; *Slam Dunk! Science Projects With Basketball* by Robert Gardner and Dennis Shortelle (Enslow Publishers, 2009)

The Lance Armstrong Performance Programme by Lance Armstrong and Chris Carmichael (Rodale, 2003) Aimed squarely at cyclists, but there's plenty of information here for all endurance athletes, including on sports science, preparation, training aims, and nutrition.

Sports Science by various authors (Franklin Watts, 2009) A series that takes a look at popular sports, such as football and tennis, and the science behind them.

Sports Science: Why Science Matters by Andrew Solway (Heinemann Library 2009)

Our Bodies by Steve Parker (Wayland, 2006) This series provides the essential knowledge about anatomy you need as a sportsperson.

WEBSITES TO VISIT

www.brianmac.co.uk
Brian Mac is a senior coach for UK Athletics, the governing body for track and field in the UK. He has 40 years of experience as an endurance athlete, and over 25 years as a coach, and most of his experience is found somewhere on this exhaustive, but easy to navigate, website.

http://coachlevi.com
This site has assorted articles for cyclists, with advice on training, nutrition and more – including a great piece on why it's a good idea for male cyclists to shave their legs. The site is useful for road racers and mountain bikers.

www.outdoorswimming society.com
This is a general-interest site for people who enjoy swimming outdoors. There is useful information for outdoor endurance swimmers, on the drop-down menu under the SWIMMING TIPS button.

Index

TRAINING FOR SPORT

Contents of titles in series: